Memoir

of a

Dead Woman

narrative poems by

Barbara Fleming Phillips

Finishing Line Press
Georgetown, Kentucky

Memoir

of a

Dead Woman

Publisher: Leah Maines

Editor: Christen Kincaid

Cover Art: Janet Shedd

Author Photo: Kam Jackson

Cover Design: Elizabeth Maines McCleavy

Printed in the USA on acid-free paper.
Order online: www.finishinglinepress.com
         also available on amazon.com

Author inquiries and mail orders:
Finishing Line Press
P. O. Box 1626
Georgetown, Kentucky 40324
U. S. A.

In memory of Viktori

For my mother and other women of
"The Greatest Generation."

August 18, 2010

7:35am

They woke me from a dream today.
I was floating in the ocean
and half sick from bobbing up and down.
The hot sun
beat against my forehead.
My lips were parched.

I thought there was a lifeboat
but every time I looked down—nothing.
Only darkness, emptiness
and a vast deep.
I began falling and jerked myself up.
I was back in the water, bobbing
up and down with the waves. Quietly,
my name was called. A rescue ship must be near.

It called again and then I woke to see
the girl with dyed black hair and crooked teeth
leaning over me. "Let's get you out of bed
for breakfast"
she said. Three of them lifted me
into my wheelchair
and put a tray in front of me.
Did they notice how hot I am? Burning up.

7:43am

My back aches
as if two great, knuckled fists
push against my flesh beneath the shoulder blades.
My head is heavy. I can't hold it up.
Farther and farther down I slide
until the white cloth tying me to the wheelchair
cuts off my circulation. My hands and arms
are swollen, tingling and asleep.
I wish I could sleep.

8:02am

I can feed myself—at least I can still do that.
But not today. I don't want oatmeal
or toast or even coffee. I just want
to sleep. I want to go home.

I can barely remember
what home looked like. The last place
I lived with Frank was a small apartment.
That building with all the other old people.

Judy and my granddaughter Allison and her husband
moved us in. It had a small back porch
and looked out over a garden
where people grew vegetables. There were sunflowers
in the distance, just peeking over
a line of forsythia. A yellow
hedge in spring and yellow faces watching me
all summer long. Squirrels were everywhere.

Before that, our house on Taylor Street.
Two stories with a grandfather clock
on the landing. Frank and I raised
two children there.

Before that, the apartment
where we lived when we first married.
And before that, Mama and Daddy's farm house.
That was really home.

8:19am

The pain is getting worse.
All over my stomach now.
It started down below.
Pain and cramps. Cramps like a school girl,
right before the monthly visitor.
Oh, that visitor—how fickle.

Just there at first, then I prayed every month
to see it come. No big belly please—
I have my life to live.

Later I wanted it, needed it.
The thick red flow.
Thick and fertile, please God, I want my children.
I knew they would be my life. Then it was gone.
Dried up, parched and useless. No longer able
to satisfy any man's
thirst for life.

8:42am

The tray is gone. I couldn't eat.
I wonder if they noticed.
I am still so hot.
I feel sick.

8:51am

This window in my room faces East.
The red gingham curtains remind me
of the tablecloth in cousin Mardi's kitchen.

She grew up with Mama, they were just like sisters.
We would visit her in the big white frame house
on the corner. It had a front porch
with two rockers
and a swing. My cousin Missy and I sat together
on the swing and walked back
until our toes
just touched the gray clapboard floor.
Then we let go and flew in that swing
with the old rusty chain
singing to us the whole ride.

Last time I saw Missy
she had just put Gene in a place like this.
He was so confused, he didn't even know her
or their kids. She was thinking about moving
just to be near him. I hope I don't get like that
where I don't even know
my own Judy.

9:03am

A bird feeder
with a red lady bug painted on top
has been hung outside my window.
They don't fill it very often
but the birds still come.

A tiny tufted titmouse flew by the other day.
"Enjoy your flight to who knows where—
enjoy your freedom" I said to it.

I'd like to fly away.

9:15am

I am sliding
in my seat. Uncomfortable wetness
rubs. I am raw.
It burns.
So much pain in my back,
so sick at my stomach.

9:24am

My feet dangle and my toes
just touch the floor. Slippers
hang from my cold feet. My legs are stiff
and painful. Unable to bear the weight
of my body for so many years.
Since just after Frank died.

It was late on a Saturday. A cold, January day.
The skies were gray with heavy snow clouds.
Frank called out to me "you"
but never finished. I shuffled to the bedroom
as fast as I could but he was gone. One arm
dangled off the bed. His brown eyes open,
stared past me toward the corner where the blue wall
met the white ceiling.

The ambulance came.
They carried him out the front door
feet first and pushing on his chest.
Neighbors stared. The ground was too cold
to bury him
for two weeks.

His brother John
who we hadn't seen in thirty years
came to say goodbye. A little too late.
I never knew why they stopped talking.
"We just don't see eye to eye," was all Frank said.
I think it might have been the way John left home.
He packed up and left Frank
to care for the whole family farm.
John didn't come home when their father died.
The old man was hard on them—hit them
to teach them a lesson. Made him into a man
Frank said, but I don't think John
ever forgave him.

Judy was home for the funeral. My precious
granddaughter Allison came too. I wish
I could have seen Allison more
when she was growing up, but Judy
needed to get away. Get away from her father
who was always finding something wrong
and from all that had happened to her.
Get away from me too,
I suppose.
Judy had so many bad days
when she was married. I guess her husband
couldn't put up with her ups and downs.
She wouldn't accept help from me—from anyone.

What a beautiful woman
Judy's daughter, Allison, has become.
I would give anything
to see Allison and her children
just one more time. I hope Judy will visit soon.
Maybe she'll bring pictures.

9:40am

That brown skinned girl
with the crisp pink uniform
who smells like rosewater has come for me.
She has left me in the hall
while they make my bed. I hate
when they roll me up against the wall
in this dark hallway behind somebody else
in a wheelchair. We are all lined up.
Old bodies and old minds. They treat us all
the same.
We will never get out.
None of us will ever get out.

9:59am

I am burning up—so hot.
I don't want to think about really burning up.
How horrible it must be.
It makes me sick.
No escape. Nobody coming to help.
Maybe they won't help me either.

10:12am

Sweat clings to my forehead
and around my hairline. My head
is heavy. Most days
strings of spit join my mouth to my gown,
but not today. Now my mouth, juiceless
with lips cracking, cannot even give me
a swallow. My rapid breaths
just make it worse.

I've known these breaths before—
rapid with sickness or with fright.
On The River Day I breathed this way,
frightened to death he would drown.

Jimmy was playing with his friends.
They were ten or eleven years old. He swung out
over the rain swollen river, green and muddy
and dropped from a tire swing.
He didn't come up.
His friends ran for help. Took almost an hour
to get four men from the gas station
down to the river.

We called the police.
About the time they showed up, he was spotted
hundreds of yards down the river
clinging to a branch.
By the time I got there, they were pulling him out
but my mind had already flashed to a picture—
his grave and his headstone
That would come later. He was safe then.
I was never the same.

10:25am

The sweet girl who smells like rosewater
noticed I don't feel well
as she pushed me to my room.
The cool washcloth on my forehead is soothing.

Some people are just kind
even when they don't have to be.

Old lady Foster's nurse was that way.
That old lady wouldn't let kids in the yard
or anybody near her. After she got sick,
not even family would visit.

Lucky for her, she had a lot of money.
She hired a nurse but was so mean, the first one quit.
Then she hired Miss Ella who was dark skinned
and real quiet. Heard Mrs. Foster
threw things at her
but Ella never gave up.
Toward the end, she stayed in that house
with Mrs. Foster day and night, even though
she didn't have to. Sat with the family
at the funeral.

11:16am

I must have dozed off.
I was dreaming of the heat. It seemed so real.
The darkness and the smoke made it hard to see.
They were screaming. I could see
their mouths moving
but I couldn't hear them scream.
Nobody could hear them.
I am so hot.

11:28am

They have pushed me down the long hall
again. This time to the big room
with windows and the loud TVs and people
who all look like me
tied into wheelchairs around the edge.

The ride has made me dizzy.
My back still hurts.
I feel sick.
They have left me here.

11:34

This dizziness feels like
when the children were small.

Jimmy was at kindergarten. Judy was home.
She must have been about two.
We were having a tea party on the living room floor
with the Blue Danube tea set mother had sent.
The dizziness hit. The room began to move
and became dim. I thought I would faint.
I was about eight weeks along
and had just found out. Frank pretended
to be happy, but I knew he was worried about money.
Business at the gas station was slow.
We had bills to pay.
I grabbed Judy and crawled on my hands and knees
to the front door. I told her if I went to sleep
to run next door and get Sadie. But I made it
next door scooting and crawling across the lawn.
Judy's laugh might have been the only thing
that kept me from passing out.
Sadie called Frank at work.
When we got to the hospital, the bleeding
was heavy. I don't remember much.

After coming home, I stayed in bed
for almost a month.
My child was gone.
My sister, Ellen, came every day. She fixed dinner
and straightened the house.
She opened my shades and made small talk.
Filled me in on the town gossip
and pushed my hair back off my face
the way mother used to do.
But it didn't help.
Nothing could pull me out of that place
until I heard Judy's little voice downstairs
crying for me, and I got up.

After that, Frank's embrace was comforting
and sympathetic. I waited for more
but could feel the distance and coolness.
I knew he didn't want any more children.
Didn't seem to want me anymore either.
From then on we drifted apart.

11:50am

That TV is loud
but at least there is laughter.
TV shows are the only time
we hear laughing.
Except on Sundays.

After church,
visitors come who laugh
a laugh of obligation fulfilled.
Of relief
at being able to leave.

11:52am

I see only four men
in this place. Funny, how women
live so much longer than men.
I had Frank longer than some wives
have their husbands.

Things had been so good at first.
I waited for him during the War. I wrote
every day.
He left with the others from home that summer—
Joe, Tony and Bill.

Dorothy and Bill had married, just like us
in the summer of 1943 before they all shipped out.
Dorothy's dad was sick but she wanted
him to give her away so she and Bill married
at the Second Presbyterian Church.
Dorothy borrowed a wedding gown
from her aunt and looked beautiful.
Bill was in the Marines. He wrote when he could.
Her dad died the next winter and she stopped
hearing from Bill that spring. Poor Dorothy.
Peggy and I tried to comfort her—
keep her spirits up.
We walked to her house after work,
played Gin Rummy and listened to the radio.
She seemed to know all along
how it would end. Dorothy lost Bill in Guam,
July of 1944. She kept that flag in a case
in the living room even after she remarried.
Dorothy never had children. I hope Dorothy
is well. I would love to see her. I wish
I could see her. I'd like to get up
from this chair, strong as ever,
and walk to see Dorothy.
I would just like to feel better.

12:08

My hands are so weak.
These hands were strong and useful before.
Mama taught me to play the piano
with these hands, and I taught Judy.
I rolled out biscuits on the dough board
at the farmhouse with Grandma. I rocked two
crying babies with these hands. I touched one more
in my belly who could never be rocked.
But these hands should have helped. Helped more,
done more that night. It haunts me.

The pain is coming in waves all around my back
and stomach. I feel sick and hot.
Hot inside and cold outside. I am dizzy.
My head hurts.

12:21

A young man and a girl
with a blond ponytail in white outfits
have pushed me to my room.
I tried to tell them my stomach hurts
and my back hurts, but my mouth is so dry
I can't get the words out.

They spoke of how many trays
and how many more pills. They didn't know
my name. They have rolled the wheelchair
next to the bed and put the tray in front of me.
Pimento cheese, apple sauce
and some kind of soup.
I can't eat.

When I was sick
Mama always made chicken and rice soup.
She let me sleep all day
on the crimson sofa with claw feet,
read stories to me and sang.
She brushed back my hair with her loving hand,
placed a cool cloth on my head
and I slept.

One winter I was quarantined.
Too young to really understand
and sick from fever and joint aches.
I was not able to walk.
My sister Ellen and brother Edward
weren't allowed in.
I heard their laughter in the house,
too weak to even care.
Aunt Martha and Mama
were the only ones I saw for months.
They read stories from books and told tall tales
of the family. Fever fueled vivid dreams
of a large dark house,

open fields of horses running
and endless swimming in a huge pond
in the heat of summer.
The water was clear and blue
like a swimming pool. Deeper and deeper
I sank. But at least I slept.
If only I could sleep now. I'd love to sleep—
really sleep.

1:05pm

The girl in white took the tray away.
She didn't notice I couldn't eat.
She was busy talking to someone about an old man
who died last night. Found him in his bed.
Pneumonia they thought.
She has left me here.
Alone.

1:14pm

I see my dresser across the room.
It is the only thing I brought from home
when Judy and Allison moved me here
after Frank died. I can barely see the photos
on top of the dresser. There is one of Frank
from the War and one of Jimmy.
I didn't want one in his uniform. I wanted
the picture of him leaning against that old Chevy.
He was so proud of that thing.
And Judy, of course. There's a picture of Judy
and a small one
of Allison and her husband and babies.

That dresser has seen a lot of moves.
Frank and I bought it when we first
started keeping house in 1943.
Paid eight dollars for it, and that was a lot.
We moved it into our apartment in town
and then to our house on Taylor Street.
I kept my jewelry
in the top drawer along with my slips
and nylons and garter belts.
Sweaters were in the middle drawer.

Judy loved to play dress up
with the things in that dresser. I didn't let her
open the box in the bottom drawer.
It held my high school class ring, Mama's rosary,
Daddy's pocket watch and
the letter from Tippy that I only read once.
I wonder if Judy will understand
if she reads that letter when I'm gone.
If she does, I wonder if she can still love me.

1:48pm

I am so very hot. I feel dry now
not sweaty any more. They have put me
back in bed, like every afternoon.
My back is burning.
I pray for sleep. I want to go home.
Home to see Mama
in her cotton dress and apron
in the old farm house. Happy and singing
like in the early days.
The days before Daddy got sick.

They said he must have caught something
but I knew better. I was fifteen, after all.
He smelled of whiskey
and stayed in his room.

Mama waited on him hand and foot.
One day, they called for Doctor Moore.
The whiskey stopped. Daddy turned yellow.
He became nice and kind and gentle.
Moaning came from his room day after day.
I ran outside to the rope swing
on the burr oak that I'd played on as a child.
I pretended he was well again.

On a Friday night in June, the moaning stopped.
He was gone. Daddy died at home.
They took him to the funeral parlor
at the top of the hill.
I didn't want to look in that coffin
but Mama said I'd be sorry if I didn't say goodbye.
He lay there in a black suit
skin, yellow as a squash
with a black rosary wound around his waxy hands.
I touched him with my fingertips.
I touched death, not Daddy.

I wished him a good life
in his new home.
I want to go home.

2:17pm

I can't sleep.
Every time I drift off, I see it. Flames
and the car. I didn't move my arms then
and I can't move them now.
It is hard to get a deep breath.
I am cold, shaking.

Did any of them notice how cold I am—shivering.
The pad beneath me is dry. My stomach hurts.
All around the back
and front. I'm hot inside
and cold outside.
My head hurts.

2:22pm

My hands are freezing. I still have
my wedding band. When we married,
Frank took my hand in his
and placed this golden band on my finger.
We promised all those things
'til death do us part.

In such a hurry to wed and go to War.
Back then, men didn't wear a wedding ring.
His hands were simple and strong
with the nicks and cuts
of a mechanic. Frank had studied
a year in college. He wanted to be a doctor
but the War came and he joined the Army.
Never went back to school after that
even though I wanted him to. He thought
he should buy the gas station
when Mr. Leary sold it. He worked hard
with those hands. They never hit me, but fingers
pointed and shook with blame. His hands
grabbed and threw and broke things.
They grasped the steering wheel of our '49 Chevy
and drove away, but he always came back.
Those hands circled around my waist, pulled me
close and we started over.

2:38pm

I want to sleep.
To go
to sleep.
I'm so hot,
burning hot.
I'm on fire.
Let me go.

2:40pm

The pain has spread to my upper back.
It goes around both sides
and down.
Just like labor pain.
I labored and labored with Jimmy
for twenty four hours, begging for help.
He was born on Monday at noon
but the bleeding wouldn't stop.
I prayed not to die. I could hear his cries
and wept myself, bargaining with God
to let me stay.
I'll be a good person if I can just live
to see my baby boy.

The doctors said I shouldn't have another
but back then, we didn't have much choice.
The next delivery was easier.
Her labor was just six hours
and I don't remember most of it—
'twilight sleep' they called it.

There should have been one more
but it ended almost as soon
as it began.

2:58pm

The sweet young rosewater girl
and the boy in white
have lifted me out of bed
and put me back in the wheelchair.
I think they know
I don't feel well. I heard them say
something about a doctor.

3:03pm

My feet are tingling.
They are swollen, puffy
and dangling here.
I haven't walked in years.
I loved to walk—all over town.
I pushed the baby carriage up the hill
to the cathedral
to see the stained glass window
of the Virgin Mary and the crucifix
with the twelve foot high Jesus.
Aunt Addie, who was married to the Church
prayed the rosary every morning.

Next to the cathedral
is the cemetery.

On that hill, everybody waits for me
under the white oak tree
where roots push up the edge
of Uncle Andrew's headstone.

He was barely out of school when the flu
swept across the country.
Mama thanked the Lord I wasn't born yet,
but Uncle Andrew caught it.
They said we lost four hundred
in our town alone.
He stayed in bed almost a month.
Couldn't eat. Crazy with fever.
Called out to people who didn't exist
then quietly, almost blessedly
went to sleep.

On that hill, they all wait
even my boy.

3:11pm

Jimmy, we thought you wouldn't have to go.
I prayed you wouldn't have to go.
You'd started college here in town,
had plans and a girlfriend.
You studied hard.
But your number was low.

It was 1968 and you were happy to go—willing to go.
Always ready for a challenge, like
on The River Day.
No fear. Each and every day of your life
was packed with going and doing and giving
and living as if you really knew
it would all be so short.

They said it came fast. You never knew.
The Captain in his crisp green uniform
looked right in my eyes and told me. Not a muscle
in his face moved. I could tell he'd done this
a hundred times. Your father
clutched my hand, your sister and I
wept and screamed. I don't even remember
the rest of that day and the next few days.
Neighbors came by and didn't know what to say.
Some of them just cried and some tried
to act like everything would be okay.
Timmy Scott visited. He told us he heard
from his cousin in Vietnam
that your company got mowed down.
A surprise attack. Shot
like a bunch of wild animals. Fourteen men dead
in one day. But as the Captain said, it was quick.

Judy and I hugged your flag-draped
coffin. Your dad stood motionless.
Emotionless. Later that day
after family and friends and that pretty blond

girlfriend with green eyes you left behind
had gone, he wept.

Never before had I seen it and never
saw it again. He sat in the old green chair
in the corner of our bedroom, head in his hands
and cried. Sobbing unselfconsciously
until I touched his shoulder.
He pulled away.
We grieved separately
and unendingly.

The letters you wrote from Vietnam
were always a comfort to me.
At least I know you were fine until the sudden end.

I kept your letters in a wooden box
in the hall closet. I guess Judy
found them when she cleaned the place out.
I hope she kept them.
Oh, Jimmy, how I would love
to see you.

3:35pm

My blue and white gown is wet again with sweat.
I am chilling.
What has happened to my clothes?
For as long as I can remember,
I've only worn bathrobes and nightgowns.
It's been years since I was dressed—
really dressed to go out
in a little black dress with a string of pearls
and black leather pumps.
And where is my jewelry?
That string of pearls from great-grandmother
and the diamond solitaire from grandmother?
Judy must have them.
That blue-eyed daughter of mine.

She played alone when she was little.
I heard her singing to her baby dolls
through the bedroom door.
She always pretended the daddy was gone.
Later, she played with Barbie and Ken.
We worried about her in high school.
She ran around with boys who had hair
down to their shoulders and came home
smelling like pot.
Judy never thought she was as good as her brother—
he did everything right.
Didn't think we loved her as much.
But she took it hard when Jimmy died,
maybe as hard as Frank and me.

I wish she would come visit.
She doesn't live that far away
but it might as well be half-way
across the world. I just don't see her enough.
Maybe she is busy painting.

Judy's paintings are majestic.

From the time she was a little girl
she could find the essence
of every creature and person and thing
laying it out beautifully in drawings
for the world to know.

When she was eleven, she won first place
in an art contest. She had drawn a picture
of our family.
We lived in a circus.
Frank was the lion tamer, Jimmy was the fire eater
she was a clown with a painted on happy face,
I was a person in the crowd.
They said she had talent. I miss her.
I want to see her.

4:03pm

I need to move, but I can't scoot up.
My body is heavy and I am weak. My hands
are tingling.

That day I had the stroke
my hands tingled. Then my face tingled
and I couldn't move my right hand.
I had trouble talking. I stretched out
on the couch. The phone rang
but I couldn't seem to reach it.
It rang again and again.
I must have blacked out.
Then, there were people in my house
bending over me. "Squeeze my hand"
they kept saying.

Next thing I knew
I was in the hospital. Judy was there with me.
She stayed almost a week. It was the most time
we had spent together
in a long time.
Her daughter, Allison, and that handsome
great grandson of mine, Jim, came too.
With those pale brown eyes
and strong chin
he is a double for my Jimmy when he was that age.
I wish he could have seen him.

My right arm got better
with all the therapy
but I still couldn't walk well.
With the stroke and back and leg problems
I would be better off
they explained
to go where someone could watch me,
where I would have help
if I fell. I wouldn't have to cook

or worry about money or shopping
or driving myself to the doctor.
Maybe I would get back home
if I got stronger. Maybe.

I don't feel strong now. I don't think I'll ever
get back. I want to go home.
And I don't think my Judy
will come unless I am really sick.

4:14pm

They don't seem to notice
how bad I feel.
Hot then cold.
My hands are numb.
I am dizzy,
almost floating.
Maybe Judy will come today.

4:18pm

Since her divorce, my Judy
rarely leaves the house.
She always kept to herself.
We didn't realize something might be wrong
until she was seventeen.
That year, she slept a lot.
We found notes to dead people
and scary sketches under her mattress.
We thought she was on drugs—
using pot like her friends.
Maybe we should have taken her
to a doctor.
A psychiatrist told her it might have been easier
if she had help earlier.
But we didn't know. Not back then.

She started painting that year.
Big dark paintings. Once she painted
the family cemetery with her own grave
at the very top of the hill—
death date and all.
Thank God she was wrong about that.
Then her pictures got brighter
and began to look like people
and things.
She slept a lot less.
She was so up and down.
We figured it was all just teenage
moods. One day crying and the next day
talking loud and laughing. Hugging everyone.

I guess we should have noticed,
but that young band director seemed so nice.
Judy played the clarinet
and she was good.
Frank was so proud of her, we all were.
It made sense that she stayed after school

to practice. I didn't know.

She came home early one day
and had been crying. Her face was flushed.
Said she was quitting band. When Frank found out
he was furious. Called her a quitter.
Said it was the only thing
she ever did well.
She wouldn't talk to me. But I knew. I knew
in my heart what had happened.
When she quit band, Frank
wouldn't let her live it down. She could never tell him
the real reason. Maybe she was afraid
of what he might do or maybe
she was really afraid if he knew what happened
he would somehow think
it was all her fault. We never talked about it.
Times were different. People never brought up
things like that. We just let it drop.
My poor, sweet Judy. I should have helped her more
but I didn't know how.

4:41pm

They have pushed me in front
of my window again.
I can hardly bear the pain in my back
and stomach.
I couldn't see who came for me. They pushed
from behind and didn't say a word.
Maybe they have gone to find a nurse.

It is raining outside. Rain would feel so good.
I love a thunderstorm and a hard
drenching rain. I didn't even mind
it rained on our wedding day.
It was small and planned in a hurry—
like most weddings in 1943.
I worked at the insurance company
the year after high school. Frank was taking
college classes and working on his family farm
for the two years he'd been out.
We'd go to the movies on Saturday night
and share a Coke float at the drugstore.
Frank was so shy,
I guess if the War hadn't come along
he never would have proposed.
All the boys in town were leaving
for the War that summer. We were married
by Judge Carter at the courthouse on a Wednesday
afternoon. No time for a church wedding.
I don't think Mama ever forgave me
for not getting married in the Catholic Church.
But Frank's people were Baptist, and there was no
time. My sister Ellen, and her husband David
stood up with us. I wore a single white orchid
on a pale green linen suit.
Mama let me borrow her string of pearls.
We ate dinner at Mama's house then Ellen and David
let us use their apartment above the shoe store
on Main Street for our wedding night.

There was no Victrola, so Frank hummed
"Moonlight Cocktail" and we danced all evening.
We were both so scared.
He promised me someday we'd have a real honeymoon.
But it was fine that we never did.

4:59pm

I'm dizzy and can't see well.
The room is dim.
My back hurts
and now my chest is hurting.
I think the young man
helping me into bed
has noticed I don't feel well.
He may have gone to find someone
to help.

5:03pm

Three or four people
surround my bed. A small tube
blowing air in my nose
only makes my mouth more dry.
I am so hot.
So hot, and sorry.
I deserve to be hot.
Please forgive me.
I was young.

It was the summer after high school
and Frank and I had not started dating.
I was out with Tippy.
Mama had forbidden me
to go with Tippy—his father was a Jew.
He had moved from back East to practice law
and was the only Jew in our little town.
Mr. Levin married a Christian woman
and nobody was quite sure
what that made Tippy.
We had run in the same crowd in high school.
Tippy was the class clown and had a heart
full of love. He did anything for anybody.
People didn't have much
and things weren't fair
in 1942. He did what was needed
and never talked about it. That heart
is why he could never get over
what happened that night.

A couple of weeks after graduation
there was a party in the country
at the Taylor farm. Tippy's family was leaving
the next day for New York.
His father had the car ready
and refused to let him take it out.
Tippy wanted to see Betty Wilson

and talked me into going to the party with him.
I told Mama I was walking up to Clara's
and Tippy sneaked the car out while his father
was busy. Mama would have disowned me—
not only out with Tippy, but alone in a car
with a boy in the country.
Everyone was drinking, including Tippy. It was
the first time I tasted whiskey.
Tippy talked to Betty
who agreed to go out with him
when he got back. I had to be home
and we were already late. About a mile
down the road as we pulled around a sharp curve
he swerved to miss something—a form
just at the edge of the dark two lane road
where the shoulder dropped off sharply
down to Mill's Creek. We looked back to see a man
looking toward the creek. Two wheels of a car
on its side were visible on the hillside. Smoke
was coming from the car. We weren't even supposed
to be out. And we had been drinking.
Besides, someone else would come along
in just a few minutes. Everyone
was leaving the party.
He didn't look hurt. Someone would give him a ride
to town and everything would be fine. Tippy
let me off at the corner, got his father's car
back in the garage
and left for New York the next morning.

News travels fast in a small town,
especially bad news. It was all anyone
talked about the next morning
and for weeks. Mr. and Mrs. Clagett—
Bobby and Margaret's parents—

were driving home from a friend's farm.
Mr. Clagett lost control of the car
on the curve and it flipped. He
was thrown out, but went back
to get Mrs. Claggett. When the car caught fire,
they were both killed. Burned to death.
Out in the country with no one to help.
By the time someone came upon the wreck
it was too late.

When Tippy got back from New York
and heard the news, he stayed in his house
for a week. When he came out, he had changed.
Said there wasn't anything
we could do about it now.
When I brought up Bobby and Margaret
going to live with their aunt, he just looked away.
He planned to join the army as soon as he could.
Wanted to go to Europe and fight the Nazis.

Tippy lived in New York after the War.
He married and divorced. Had a daughter
about Judy's age.
I saw him when his father died. That's when
he gave me the letter.
I only read it once.

5:35pm

I've been hot all day
    but now I am so cold
people keep coming in my room
they all touch my arms
    and push on my belly
pain has spread
    into my chest
pressure in my chest
    is unbearable
such a heaviness
    I can barely breathe
pressure in my chest
    is squeezing

the girl in pink
    is leaning over me
she has a beautiful face
she looks like Judy
she looks like Mama
there are lights around her head
    shining from behind
she looks afraid

I can't get air
I don't want her to worry
I am feeling better
I can go to sleep now
she is running from the room

5:37pm

she is back and has brought others
I hear them calling my name
  but the sound
  is getting farther
  and farther away
can barely see
  what is going on around me
everything is hazy
my arms and legs are light
the pain is gone

Drums beat in the distance—a soft and constant sound. I am light and comfortable. Weightless, floating. Floating above myself. I see clearly now. I see my bed and my body on the bed. I see the curtains that look like cousin Mardi's and the dresser and the pictures of Judy and Frank and Jimmy. There are people leaning over me. They are touching my chest and my belly. They don't know I can't feel them. I want to tell them I'm alright. Soft flute music is above me, calling me—no, pulling me up, away from my body and this room. Through the building and into the air, into what must be the sky. I see trees, full with leaves and the top of the building I am in. I see the road that leads to town and cars. Now I can see the river. If I follow it along—yes—there's our old house on Taylor Street and the lot where Frank's gas station used to be and the school and the church and the graveyard. There's the road out of town that leads to Mama and Daddy's farm. It is all so far away now. I am floating into yellow. I am tumbling—tumbling out of control, but not afraid. Tumbling in yellow space. It is darkening to a yellow-brown and my tumbling is slowing. What was air is now a substance—as it thickens, I slow until I am still. Stuck in a brown substance that surrounds me completely. Fear is rising. Fear and terror. But beyond me in the thickness, I sense a familiar presence, the presence of someone I know. Not a physical form, but a presence, an energy that is so familiar to me. A changing globe from brown to yellow lights in the substance and my fear is gone. I am not alone. The energy from this bright orb, a familiar presence cuts through the darkness to touch me and I know it as Jimmy. We are reunited. We are one. We are absolute love. As his energy moves away beyond me, it cuts a path through the thick brownness.

Beyond the substance, I see comforting, clear blue in the opening he has made. Another presence calls to me and lights the darkness. This orb of energy reaches to me through the darkness and I am reunited with Mama. We are self-sacrifice. We are absolute love. As she leaves, another opening to the blue beyond is made. A light is now lit in the brown and sluggish substance that is somehow heavier than the other orbs and less familiar. Its brightness is quicker and its impact more severe. This energy connects with me and I know it as Mr. and Mrs. Claggett. We are forgiveness. We are absolute love. As they leave, an opening in the murkiness once again appears. The clear blue beyond is becoming more apparent. Fear is waning. A small light appears as a glowing orb and touches me quickly. I know it though I have never known it, and I have always known it. Somehow it is sorrow and joy at the same time and we are whole. We are innocence. We are absolute love. In turn, each one I knew who has gone before me reaches out in light and energy. Each with its own message of compassion or understanding, of faithfulness or trust, but always of love—absolute love. This is a process of patience, each taking its own time to reach out and reunite and yet it all happens in an instant and I am left floating in the clear, profound blue space they have made for me. I am joyous. All is peace in this vast blue. I am weightless, I am buoyant, this could be eternity, yet I am drawn to a circle of darker blue in the distance. It draws me like a magnet. I am sucked into a hole moving faster than I have ever known. Rushing through a length of deep blue-black, I am released into a magnificent pool of indescribable color. Formless beings float in the pool of color in every direction. Each is shimmering and luminous with a brightness and power about it. These collections of light are individual, yet each of us is the same. Unique, yet identical. My understanding surpasses all. Nothing is a mystery. All is known. I am the knowing. I am.

Born and raised in Frankfort, Kentucky, **Barbara Fleming Phillips** graduated from Centre College and Wright State University School of Medicine. She spent time in Ohio before returning home to Kentucky. She resides in Lexington, where she practices medicine. Her poetry is informed by attention to detail honed through her background in the sciences. She draws inspiration from the events and lives of people around her. Her poems have appeared in *The Binnacle, Calliope, The Heartland Review, JAMA* and others and her chapbook *Early Lessons* was published in 2009.

www.ingramcontent.com/pod-product-compliance
Lightning Source LLC
Chambersburg PA
CBHW070551090426
42735CB00013B/3154